Kerr Boyce Tupper

Diaz

The Apostle of Cuba

Kerr Boyce Tupper

Diaz
The Apostle of Cuba

ISBN/EAN: 9783337381899

Printed in Europe, USA, Canada, Australia, Japan

Cover: Foto ©Lupo / pixelio.de

More available books at **www.hansebooks.com**

THE APOSTLE ~~OF CUBA~~

KERR BOYCE TUPPER, D. D.

PHILADELPHIA

AMERICAN BAPTIST PUBLICATION SOCIETY

1420 Chestnut Street

1896

DIAZ—THE APOSTLE OF CUBA

THE suggestive remark it is of Pascal that the notable men of the world's life move and shine in three distinct and glorious orbits—the orbit of heroism, the orbit of intellectuality, and the orbit of personal moral worth. As intelligent students of history we must be impressed with the many illustrations of this truth. In the first orbit we note the Cæsars, the Charlemagnes, and the Napoleons of history—men of mighty military prowess and splendid martial achievements. In the second, we mark the Platos and the Homers, the Senecas and the Bacons of the different ages—men of genuine mental worth and vast range of intellectual power. In the third sphere, standing out in consummate glory, are the Martyns, the Wilberforces, the Judsons, and the Careys of history—men whose chief excellency consists, not in heroism as the world counts the hero, nor in mere intellectuality, but rather in a sublime renunciation of self, a passionate love of God, and a Christlike devotion to the highest interests of their fellows—men who, now as missionaries, now as martyrs, now as philanthropists, now as teachers, go up and down our earth illustrating what the poet sings :

To honor God, to benefit mankind,
To serve with lowly gifts the little needs
Of the poor race for which the God-man died,
And do it all for love—ah! this is great,
And he who does this will achieve a name
Not only great, but good.

It is in this last and noblest orbit, to use the figure of our Christian philosopher, that the subject of our brief sketch, Alberto José Diaz, the consecrated Cuban missionary, has moved with such conspicuous eminence during the past ten years. The life of so heroic a spirit as his cannot fail both to interest and to instruct.

The chief purpose of this monograph, however, being to present Diaz in connection with his Christian work as a Baptist missionary in Havana, as the devoted apostle to Cuba, we must content ourselves with a mere outline of his history preceding and leading up to the great mission of his life. To many the history of this wonderful man is as fascinating as it is instructive. He was the eldest son of a devoted mother, who surely was as a fruitful vine, since he had no fewer than twenty-four brothers and sisters. He received his early education at home and in fitting schools and, at great expense on his father's part, a liberal training at the University of Havana both as an academic and medical student. Up to this time he had never seen a Bible, notwithstanding his access to the best public and private libraries of the island. He was successful in his practice as a physician in his native country. His heroism and courage as captain among the insurgents are still remembered. Narrowly escaping from drowning when floating on a plank in the sea to get away from pursuing foes, who had slain all but three of his companions, he was rescued, after twenty-six hours' drifting, by a fishing vessel, and safely borne to New York City. Through exposure, pneumonia came upon him in Brooklyn and an almost fatal illness followed. Prayers for and with him were offered by a devout Christian woman, who took a deep interest in his temporal and spiritual welfare, and recovery came. With it there came the possession of new gospel light, which his soul had gotten from talking with the noble woman, who had read the Scriptures to him and agonized with God for his recovery, both of body and spirit. In total, affectionate self-surrender, he gave himself to Jesus Christ as personal Master and Redeemer, and returned to Cuba—the rebellion being over and amnesty proclaimed. His whole soul was aflame with enthusiasm to declare the good tidings of great joy to all the people in that blighted, priest-ridden land, although his reward in part was persistent and cruel persecution by priests and other enemies of the true faith. Even his own mother rejected him, although afterward she became, and is to-day, a devoted co-laborer with her son in the gospel. He soon returned to Brooklyn, which was still fragrant with the memories of a godly woman and the presence of the Holy Spirit. At the Calvary Baptist Church, New York City, he witnessed with his sister the first apostolic baptism his eyes had ever beheld, and deep conviction of its biblical truth fastened itself upon him. His own

baptism followed soon afterward, about thirteen years
ago, in Gethsemane Baptist Church, Brooklyn, upon
glad confession of personal trust in our once buried and
now risen and exalted Christ, his sister Minnie having
preceded him in this duty. His appeal to our American Baptist Home Mission Society to send him as missionary to Cuba was declined because of lack of funds,
and he was accepted by the Women's Bible Society in
Philadelphia as missionary to Cuba, and departed in
1883 for that land, for whose redemption he constantly
and earnestly prayed and pined. His spiritual solitude
there among the ignorant, idolatrous adherents of
Rome ; his earnest endeavors to disseminate the Scriptures, both as oracle of faith and manual of devotion ;
his arrest and imprisonment by the police as a possible
conspirator ; his songs and prayers, like those of Paul
and Silas, in prison, and their holy influence upon his
fellow-prisoners ; his appeal as an American citizen for
release, and its speedy attainment ; the organization by
him and his friends of the "Society for Religious Wor-
ship," which, however, for safety against native influence, was changed to "Reformed Church of Cuba" ;
the futile demand by the priests and bishops of the
Episcopal Church to draw this new organization into
their fraternity ; the firm, intelligent determination of
Diaz and his co-laborers to organize themselves into a
regular apostolic Baptist church, based upon the New
Testament, and the New Testament alone, as they un-
derstood it ; his separation from the Philadelphia Bible
Society and his connection with the Home Mission

Board of the Southern Baptist Convention ; his ordination as a Baptist minister in Florida ; the conversion and baptism of his father and mother as happy believers in their Lord;—all this forms a fascinating part of the story of what has been now for years his glad and glorious, his persuasive and permanent, his God-glorifying and man-saving, work in his much-loved native land.

A most attractive spot, in some respects, is this arena of Diaz' labors, it being the largest and most fertile of the West India Islands, known first as Juana, then as Fernandine, now as Cuba. The people are naturally docile, generous, polite, far in character above the haughty, cruel, unreliable Spaniard. Romanism, however, has for centuries, and in every direction, cast its blighting, withering, and awful influence over this beautiful garden spot. As a result, the people as a class have but little knowledge of the Bible and less reverence for the Lord's Day. They are ignorant of civil liberty and religious liberty. For wherever the Spanish law has gone, as another has well said, the hand of the Inquisition has stifled liberty and conscience, and wherever Romanism has undisputed sway, manhood and womanhood have been degraded. Strangers also these Cubans are to the Christianity uncovered by human ritual, untainted by human tradition. Above all things, these Cubans need a pure, unemasculated evangel, which can relieve their consciences, illumine their intellects, redeem their spirits, transform their lives, and make them, in deed and in truth, new creations in Christ Jesus. Such an evangel Alberto Diaz

has sought now for a decade to give them in tears and
prayers, in suffering and sacrifice.

And what does this decade of toil and hardship, of
consecrated energy and devoted self-denial by this man
of God, reveal in the way of solid, substantial work for
the Master and his kingdom in Cuba?

It is hardly too much to say that few missions have
been so successful as that of Alberto Diaz. In his fascinating "Story of Diaz," Dr. G. W. Lasher gives the
following facts: "During the first fifteen months after
the organization of his church, Diaz baptized three
hundred converts, all intelligently leaving the church of
Rome and covenanting with each other to live and
labor for the redemption of Cuba from the thraldom of
Romanism. They know what they believe, and, above
all, they know why they no longer sympathize with the
church of Rome, ruled over by priests and bishops.
Among the baptized was every member of Diaz' own
family and his wife's family—seventeen in all. During
these fifteen months these people had given one thousand and seventy-eight dollars and fifty cents for the
support of their own church, eighty dollars for missions
in Florida, and two dollars to each of the Southern
Boards. They called their organization the 'Gethsemane Baptist Church,' for the church in Brooklyn,
New York, where Alberto and Minnie Diaz had been
baptized." In 1889 the Jané Theatre was purchased for Diaz' work at a cost of sixty-five thousand dollars, the original cost of the building being
one hundred and forty thousand dollars. This is a

THE GETHSEMANE BAPTIST CHURCH, HAVANA.

handsome, attractive structure, built of white stone, the inside finished with white marble, the balcony of iron enameled with white.   It is lighted throughout with electricity and gas, which gives a very pleasing effect to the auditorium.   In one part of the house we read on the walls *Dios es Amor;* on another, *Cuba para Christos.*   At the back of the platform, a baptistery has been arranged with running water, while in front, where once were footlights, is the preacher's stand.   The theatre is capable of seating about three thousand, and is situated in the busy part of the city, accessible to the residents of Havana and near the chief hotels, thus making attendance upon these services convenient to those who visit the city, among whom in winter are many Americans.

The Gethsemane Church and its branches in Havana, to which Dr. Diaz has given himself so nobly, numbers at present about two thousand six hundred and seventeen members, while fully three thousand rejoicing converts to a pure Christianity have been baptized by him and his helpers.   It is estimated that no fewer than ten thousand persons have applied for baptism at the hands of our missionary there, but he rejects many because without evidence of a regenerating and saving faith in the Son of God.   Hear his own words on this matter: "We have no difficulty in getting the people to be baptized, for as soon as they become members the first thing they ask is to be baptized.   We, of course, are obliged to use discretion as to whom we accept as members, for there are many people there

who sympathize with us, known as the anti-Catholics.
They have left the Catholic Church, but still have not
received Christ, and are not regenerated.   These are
not the people we want ; we want all our members to
be hard and earnest workers for Christ.   We keep a
book in our church, and at the end of every service we
ask all present who are not members of the congregation, but sympathize with us, to come forward and sign
the book.   There are about eight thousand names on
it now.''

And the most potential factor, humanly speaking,
in this vast and varied Christian work is the enthusias-
tic, devoted personality of Dr. Diaz himself.   One who
knows him well has put it well when he says : ''On
that morning when Diaz landed in Havana, without
money, without friends, without support, with nothing
but his Bible, determined, God helping him, to win
Cuba for Christ, it was a picture of moral heroism
never surpassed in the history of Christian devotion.
He might have uttered there and then the words of the
apostle to the Gentiles : 'I could wish myself accursed
from Christ for my brethren, my kindred according to
the flesh.'   Through all the years of his ministry his
spirit has known no abatement.   With a zeal deterred
by no dangers, faltering at no obstacles, and with a
faith in God which surmounted every trial, he has presented himself a living sacrifice to the work he has un-
dertaken ; exemplifying every Christian virtue in his
consecrated life, he has infused the same spirit into
his converts.   Such an example could not fail to exert

a controlling power over the lives of those who accept his doctrines. When they read in their Bibles of faith, courage, patience, love, devotion to duty, self-denial, whole-hearted service for Christ, they see in their great leader's life the meaning of these teachings, and they follow him as he follows Christ."

The beneficent influence of this Gethsemane Church is incalculable, felt as it is widely and deeply over the entire island. One colporter recently gave testimony that since this Baptist work began, he has sold more than thirty thousand Testaments and Bibles outside of Havana, as he made visits from door to door in the principal cities and towns of Cuba, the people speaking of the word of God as "the living light from heaven." Another Bible distributer relates that when lately on a train, coming from Havana to Matanzas, he was offering his Bibles for sale, a priest asking of him what book he was selling, being informed that it was the Scriptures, bought a copy and began to examine it. In a few moments this priest was noticed tearing the book in a hundred pieces and throwing the leaves out of the window. Some one sitting near him asked why he so treated it, and the priest replied : "It is a bad book, used only by heretics." The curiosity of the travelers was so aroused by the priest's action that the colporter immediately sold the remaining seven, God thus using the wrath of man to praise him. These are two instances only of how the word is having free course and being glorified in connection with Diaz' work in that land of superstition and spiritual dark-

ness.   Nor are these cases exceptional.   The Secretary
of the Home Mission Board of the Southern Baptist
Convention, under which Dr. Diaz prosecutes his im-
portant work, writes: "The determined efforts of the
bishop of Havana to destroy it have resulted in its in-
creased popularity and influence.   Failing in his well-
planned schemes to overthrow it, he has publicly de-
clared that Alberto J. Diaz, the superintendent of the
Baptist missions, is such a favorite with the Cuban officials, that they are unwilling to do justice to the Catholic
Church.   It is not too much to say that one-half the
population sympathize with Brother Diaz in his contest
with the bishop."

In the cemetery which Diaz years ago secured for
his Havana church, and to which the natives have given
the attractive name of "Flower Garden," there have
been sold up to the present time seventeen thousand
graves, the larger part of them being purchased by
Catholics, who can buy here a grave at a much less
cost than in the Catholic cemetery, where, besides
being high in price, the burial place belongs to the
purchaser for five years only, at the expiration of
which time, unless more money is paid, the body
buried is removed to a common receptacle and the
vacant grave used for another burial.   The sale of
cemetery lots was a source of great revenue to our
church in Havana until the Catholics, in self-defense,
were obliged to give free burial to those of their number who needed it.

Dr. Diaz has no truer nor more liberal friend and

supporter than J. S. Paine, of Cambridge, who gave to this missionary his first two hundred dollars with which to buy a burial place for his people. Under the date of April 27, he writes: "I have been interested in the Havana church from its beginning, which was about twelve years ago last June. My wife and I arrived in Havana in February of the same year. We have spent many winters in Cuba, and know of Dr. Diaz' work. We partook of the first communion service conducted by him. Most solemn and impressive it was, with doors and windows closed and the room dimly lighted for fear of trouble from those outside. Dr. Diaz is not only a preacher of the gospel, but a physician and surgeon of ability, having graduated from the medical school in Havana. Besides preaching the gospel he maintains a hospital for women and children, which has done a vast amount of good and been the means of many helpful additions to the church. The church in Havana has gone gloriously onward ever since its organization."

This testimony of Mr. Paine is corroborated by the author of the "Story of Diaz," when he says: "From the time of entering the new house, the course of the church and pastor and his fellow-helpers has been constantly onward. The new believers are taught that works must result from their faith; that they are to make sacrifices for Christ, and are to contribute according to their ability for the spread of the gospel. The treasurer of the church meets the candidate for baptism between the dressing room and the baptistery, and asks

him how much he proposed to give for the support of
the gospel. No member is retained who does not do
something. Consequently there is constant progress.
One mission station after another has been established,
and as a need of preachers and pastors has arisen, the
Lord of the harvest has provided the men for the respective fields." Even so far back as eight years ago
the work of Gethsemane Church was reported as follows: Missionaries, twenty; churches and stations,
twenty-seven; baptisms, three hundred; Sunday-
schools, twenty-six; teachers and pupils, two thousand
two hundred and twenty-eight; total membership of
the seven churches, one thousand four hundred and
ninety-three; money collected by these churches, two
thousand two hundred and fifty-five dollars and seventy
cents.

One is amused as well as touched to learn the method
of Dr. Diaz, on a certain occasion, in the selection of
deacons for his church. The account he gives speaks
volumes for the consecration of this simple-hearted,
Christ-believing, God-glorifying folk. In his own naïve
way he reports it to us. "My people," says he, "are of
a peculiarly jealous nature. If one of them is selected
to perform a duty, they think that he is in better favor
than the rest and are accordingly much hurt. This was
the difficulty which confronted me when I found it necessary for me to select the seven deacons to aid in car-
rying on the church work. I studied the problem over
for some time, and at last hit upon a plan which I
thought would work satisfactorily. One Thursday even-

ing, at the close of the services, I announced that the
next Sunday we would select the deacons, and that the
sermon would be on the duties of the deacons.   That
Sunday every member was present, and the church was
crowded.   I told them that it was the duty of the deacons when they were notified of a case of smallpox to
go immediately and attend to it ; the same if it were a
case of cholera, or in any epidemic, they must be the
first to be present and offer aid, and the last to come
away ; that they were to have their Testaments with
them always, and were to make a conversion whenever
the opportunity presented itself.   After presenting the
case in as serious a light as possible, I requested those
who felt courageous enough to assume the responsibili-
ties of the position to stand up.   The whole congregation stood up.   I knew it would be useless to attempt
to make any selections, so I said to them, 'Go ahead,
you are all deacons.'   Now they all carry their New
Testaments around with them, and telling, whenever
they have a chance, of the religion of Christ.   Thus,
you see, we have a whole congregation of workers.''
And the missionary's testimony is borne out by Dr.
Burrows, Secretary of our Southern Baptist Convention,
who writes in a sprightly tract : ''Grouped around Diaz
are those who have caught the inspiration of his high
purpose, and whom he successfully leads in the ever-
increasing and multiform demands of the work.   Under
this leadership the types of Christian activity are far
beyond the standard at which American churches are
content to rest.   There are no drones.   The week ser-

vice and the Sabbath service alike attract the whole body of disciples to the place of prayer. The singing is common to all. Even children respond when called upon with cheerful alacrity to lead the devotions of the congregation. No prolonged service wearies them or produces signs of discontent. The opportunity given at every gathering to contribute of means is accepted with cheerfulness. The eagerness and zeal of a Cuban Baptist congregation is contagious.''

And to develop this work, what persecutions this man of God, this apostle of Christ, has had to endure ! Take this one case as he himself tells of it in 1890 :

'' Last year, as I was about to start for the United States to come to the meeting at Northfield, I received an invitation to visit a town a little way from Havana to preach ; everything was in readiness. This opportunity of holding a meeting in that town was not to be lost. They had secured the theatre for the occasion, and we expected to have a large number of people present. I decided to go. When I arrived in the town I found the theatre all lighted and nearly full of people, awaiting me before commencing the services. We opened the meeting by singing a hymn, and as I arose to preach, a policeman came into the room, and said :

'' 'You cannot have your meeting here.'

'' 'Why,' said I, 'we are inside of a building, and are not breaking any law.'

'' 'This is a public building,' he replied, 'and I have orders not to allow you to hold your meeting here.'

'' We consulted among ourselves, and decided to

hold our meeting in the Baptist church. The church was a small affair, and would not hold more than fifty. On arriving there we found that nearly all the people had accompanied us, and that the edifice could not accommodate them all. The pastor of the church, however, had a large yard or court behind his house which was enclosed with high walls, and he gave us permission to have our meeting there. We accepted his hospitality, and putting up some candles in various parts of the court, opened the meeting. We sang hymns and preached, and were very happy that the Lord had at last enabled us to hold a meeting in that town. At the close of the meeting we sang the hymn, 'We will soon be at home over there,' and just as I was singing this line, a soldier, who had come into the yard unobserved, stepped up to me, and said :

" 'Yes, you will soon be at home over there ' (pointing to the jail).

" The whole congregation protested when they saw the soldiers preparing to arrest us and take us away, saying :

" 'If you take these men to jail, you must take us too.'

" We calmed the people, and told them it was best to go quietly, and all would be well. The soldiers conducted us to the house of the mayor, and showed us into his presence.

" After he had taken our names and asked the customary questions, he began to interrogate us in this way :

" 'Well, mister,' said he, turning to one of my companions, 'what have you been doing up there?'

" 'I have been reading the Bible,' was the answer given.

" 'Put him in jail for reading the Bible,' said the mayor.

" 'Now, sir, what have you been doing up there?' said he to the other.

" 'I have been praying and singing.'

" 'Put him in jail for praying and singing,' commanded the mayor.

" 'Well,' said he, turning to me, 'what have you been doing?'

" 'I have been reading the Bible and preaching the gospel,' I answered.

" 'Put him in jail for reading the Bible and preaching the gospel,' he ordered.

"And thus our three cases were disposed of, and we were taken to the jail at two o'clock in the morning, to be incarcerated among criminals and desperadoes of the worst description, for the crime of having a meeting to glorify our Lord and Saviour Jesus Christ. We said to ourselves after they had put us in our cell and left us :

" 'Well, we are here, let us hold another service and see if they will put us out for the same reason that they have put us in.' We began to sing and pray, and kept it up until five o'clock in the morning.

"Our friends in Havana, learning that we were imprisoned, notified the consul-general, requesting that he have us released, as we were American citizens and doing nothing wrong. The consul, however, was afraid of the power of the priests, and would not take any action, fearing that he might offend them. Finding that we need not expect any assistance from him, we notified our friends in New York, and Mr. J. S. Paine, of your city, asking them to render us as much aid as possible. We also telegraphed to the Secretary of State, Mr. James G. Blaine, telling him of the circumstances regarding our arrest and imprisonment and asked that he send orders for our release. Now, Mr. Blaine was not afraid of the priests, and sent a cablegram right back to the consul with instructions that he take us from the prison immediately. The consul came himself and had us released. The Cuban officials investigated our case, and at the end of nine months concluded that we had broken no law, and were innocent of any crime. They now gave us license to hold our meetings in any part of the country. Thus you may see how in these two cases the persecution worked directly for our benefit."

Among the most interesting incidents of Diaz are those connected with the conversion and baptism of his own parents. How simple it is, as told by himself five years ago in Boston. Said he, on that occasion in an address in the Clarendon Street Baptist Church :

" I immediately commenced my labors in my own family. They were astonished and troubled to hear me talking of Christ, the Bible, and salvation, and were greatly opposed to it, my mother refusing to listen to me. Every member of the family was against me, with

the exception of a little four-year-old sister, who, after
hearing of Christ, said, 'I like that Man and will love
him.' My mother was a Catholic, and very bitter
against what I said. She called me a Protestant, a
heretic, and a Jew. She said, 'I will not speak to you
if you do not come back to the church and the religion I
taught you.' I tried to tell her about Christ and his
word, but she would not listen to me; all she would
say was, 'If you are my son and love me, you will
leave that religion and come back to the Catholic
Church.' She knew very well that I loved her, and
what she said troubled me very much; we lived in the
same house for months without her speaking to me. I
trusted in the Lord, however, and prayed every night
and morning for her conversion. Within six months
she came into our congregation and became a member.
Let me tell you of the way in which it came about.
We were holding one of our evening meetings with
quite a large number of people present. I was very
much surprised to see my mother come in and take a
seat; she never attended any of our meetings. Her
presence disturbed me, as I thought she had come to
reprove me before the people, but, mastering my feel-
ings, I preached my usual sermon and then gave the invitation for those who wished to become members to
stand up. Four people arose; my mother was one of
them. Now I thought sure she was going to speak
to me. Three of the people stood on my right side,
and my mother was on the left side. Not know-
ing what she was going to do, I turned my back to her

and began to examine the other three, thinking she would think better of what she was about to do and go away. I was intently engaged with the three persons whom I was examining, when one of the brothers said:

"'Mr. Diaz, there is your mother standing over there; why don't you speak to her?' Turning to her, I said:

"'Well, mother, what are you doing here?'

"'Alberto,' said she, 'don't you want me in your church?'

"'Yes, mother, we want you if you are ready to receive the Lord Jesus Christ; but how is it that you have changed?' I asked in some surprise.

"'Through the Lord Jesus Christ, whom I have found in your Bible,' she answered.

"Then she stood up and told the people of the trouble we had had, how she had not spoken to me for so long a time, but when she had read my Bible and found the way to salvation, she could no longer resist coming and joining us.

"I examined her then, asking all the questions which I knew she had disliked to be asked. Did she still believe in the pope, the priests, and confession? She said :

"'I believe in the Lord Jesus Christ; let all those things pass, I do not care for them now.'

"When my mother was in my own hands, and I was about to immerse her, all the words that my tongue would give utterance to were—

"'Lord Jesus, this is my mother, have mercy.'

"Everything was working nicely, and we were meeting success on every hand. The only thing that troubled me was that I had been unable to convert my father. He was a man of science who, immersed in his scientific studies, thought, like many others, that religion was something good enough for women and children, but nothing for a man to have anything to do with. I approached him one day with my Bible, and said:

"'Father, don't you want to read this book?'

"'No,' said he, 'that book is too old; I want something new.'

"'Why, father, you don't know anything about it, this book is always new; in it you will find an answer for any question you may have. If it is not there, it is nowhere.'

"'Well,' he said, 'I may read it sometime.' And thus he put me off.

"It discouraged me very much, but mother and I prayed night and morning for his conversion. My little sister heard us in our prayer one morning, as we were asking the Lord to aid us in the conversion of my father, and she said:

"'Well, what are you troubled so much about father for?'

"'We want to get father to read the Bible and be converted,' I answered.

"'Do you think, Alberto, that if he reads the Bible he will be converted?' she exclaimed.

"'Yes,' I said; 'if we can only get him to read the Bible he will soon be converted.'

" 'Then I will make him read the Bible,' she exclaimed. So in about three or four days, when Sunday came, she went to him, putting on her gloves and, making him believe she was in a great hurry, said:

" 'Father, won't you please read those three or four verses for me? I am in a great hurry, and I want to know my lesson before I go to Sunday-school.' Father loves her very much, and would do anything for her, so he took her Bible and read the verses she had pointed out to him. He did not 'smell the rat,' and she, under various pretences, succeeded in keeping him reading the Bible for her. Early one morning I awoke and saw a light in my sister's room, and being afraid that she might be sick, I went in to see what was the matter. For a moment I was so surprised at what I saw that I could not speak. There sat my father reading the Bible at four o'clock in the morning. I said to him:

" 'Father, what have you been doing here?'

" 'Oh, I have been reading this book,' he answered; 'what time is it?'

" 'Four o'clock,' I told him.

" 'Four o'clock! No,' he said; 'it cannot be more than eleven.'

" But I told him it was really four o'clock, and asked how he liked the book.

" 'I like this book,' he said, 'and will go with you next Sunday.'

" He came to the church with us the following Sunday, and was baptized and received into the congregation."

A noble, philanthropic work Diaz has sought to do in establishing Red Cross stations, or "Blood Hospitals," as they are called in Cuba, for the help of the wounded and ill among the Spanish and Cuban soldiers. These hospitals are distributed, six or seven in number, throughout the center of the island where the present fighting occurs, and where the Spanish Government has about twenty thousand soldiers. Each of these stations consists of a native physician, selected from the locality where the station is situated, two Baptist women nurses, and usually about ten male helpers. Each of these stations is thoroughly equipped with medical supplies, appliances, and instruments for surgical use. Each station has assigned to it a definite territory in which it is expected to operate. The plan of operation is to move closely after the columns of troops, and when an engagement takes place the men connected with the hospital go immediately on the battleground and carry out the wounded from both armies as rapidly as possible to the hospital tent, where they receive immediate surgical and other necessary attention. Since the organization of these stations many lives have been saved which would otherwise have been lost but for prompt attention rendered to the wounded. These stations are entirely impartial between the two armies, devoting their best skill to relieving the wounded and suffering on either side. Each of the contending forces usually removes its own wounded after the battles are over, finding many of them in the tender care of the nurses at these stations and often discovering that life had been saved.

This work is greatly appreciated by the soldiers of both armies, and has also received complimentary official recognition from the government of Spain.

As far back as September of last year we read of Diaz' visit to Sagua and St. Domingo and other towns, organizing these stations. In visiting these places, our Christian hero narrowly escaped death on one occasion through a battle between the Spanish and Insurgents, and the very next day he started out again, saying: "I have made ready my satchel to leave Havana for Santa Clara and Sagua again Monday morning, and in the name of the Lord I go. He will take care of me and help me in this new organization of the work."

A short time since not only the Baptist fraternity but all American Christians were startled to learn that this devoted laborer of God and of man had been arrested and imprisoned in Havana, the Spanish authorities suspecting him of being sympathetic with the Insurgent forces in the movement for independence. It was not the first time that this affliction had come to him. Less than six years ago, in June, 1890, he, with two assistants, was imprisoned in Wianno, the Mayor of the village having them locked up in the common jail. We recall reading how the Christians and people gathered in front of the prison and threatened to mob the authorities, and would doubtless have used violence had not Diaz himself, appearing on the balcony, besought them to be peaceable and quiet. Two days and a half these Christians were imprisoned and then released. Hear our missionary's own account of the event:

" I had occasion to go to the city of Wianno, which is a short distance from Havana, to distribute some Bibles which had been sent to me by the ladies in Philadelphia, and had them in a box in the freight car. When we reached our destination, I noticed a man come into the car and talked to the passengers. I paid no attention to him, as I thought he was a baggageman. At last he reached the seat in which I was sitting, and asked if my name was Diaz.

" ' Yes, that is my name,' I answered.

" ' Then you are my man,' he said, putting his hand on my shoulder.

" ' What do you mean ? ' I asked.

" ' I am the mayor of this town,' he said, 'and I am here to arrest you.'

" I at first thought that this was a joke, and thinking to make matters smooth, I took him by the hand, and said:

" ' Why, don't you remember me; were you not an old schoolfellow of mine at the university? '

" ' No,' he answered, ' I am the magistrate of this town, and I am here to put you in jail. You must come with me.'

" Finding that it would be useless to prolong our talk, I got up and left the car with him. On the platform I found ten or twelve soldiers under arms waiting for me to escort me to jail, and then I can assure you I knew it was no joke. The magistrate asked me if there was anything in the car belonging to me. I told him that there was a box of Bibles in the freight car. He ordered the soldiers to bring the box out and put it on a team. Everything being ready, they formed their lines and put me in the center, and with the team with my box of Bibles leading the way, we started off through the town to the jail. The children followed us in the street, and the men and women came to the doors and windows of their houses to see us go by. They all wanted to see the 'filibuster man,' as I was called. When we arrived at the jail, without advising me why I was to be held, they put me in one cell and my box of Bibles in another. Sunday came, and I asked the jailer for permission to go among the prisoners and talk to them.

" ' No,' he said, ' the mayor says you are a dangerous fellow, and that I must not have anything to do with you or your book.' "

But Diaz appealed as an American citizen to the United States Consul, who at once took the matter in hand and demanded of the authorities immediate release or a trial on some specific charge. The authorities being unable to find that he had broken any laws, released him at once.

But greater excitement, however, prevailed (1896) when all over the land there was flashed along the wires that Diaz was again a prisoner for conscience' sake. To him as an American citizen, as well as one whose citizenship is in heaven, all eyes have been turned, and a commentary on his good name and widespread fame is the complimentary manner in which the secular press has spoken of this Baptist hero.

The Washington correspondent of the "Philadelphia Press" said:

There are few men more popular among the Baptists of this country than is Diaz. Since his conversion to that faith he has been prominent at their annual conferences, and his speeches and discourses have aroused enthusiasm. He has been to Washington several times. He is a little man, inclined to be fat, and looks like a Mexican. His manner is nervous and full of enthusiasm, conspicuous for that chivalry peculiar to a certain class of the Latin race. He is intensely in earnest at all times, arousing the emotions of those brought under his influence. The dash and courage which marked him as a revolutionist before he joined the mission of the church he has carried into his religious work. I am told by ministers of that church that he is regarded as the most successful of all their missionary workers. They say that what he has accomplished in Cuba is extraordinary. His earnestness and enthusiasm are contagious. An example of his influence is given in a story of his having converted and baptized his jailer while in prison. The Baptists in this country are greatly interested in his fate. The awakening of their sympathy with the Cuban cause through their interest in him is likely to result in material aid to the revolutionists. Should harm come to him, this sympathy would probably set at defiance the laws of neutrality. A minister of one of the leading churches of that denomination here said to me the other day that if Diaz were not set at liberty, there would be an army of Baptists ready to fight the battles of Cuba, and thousands would find means of joining the Cuban army.

At a special meeting of the Home Mission Board of the Southern Baptist Convention, the following resolution was unanimously adopted :

Resolved, That the Board has heard with the deepest pain of the imprisonment of Bro. A. J. Diaz by the Spanish authorities in Cuba; that we are profoundly impressed with the duty of doing all in our power to preserve the life and secure the liberty or our beloved brother; that for this purpose we invite all Baptists everywhere, and such other Christian brethren as may sympathize with us, to unite in a common effort to influence the authorities of our land to do everything consistent with the honor of our country to accomplish our wishes; that public meetings be held by them and such others as may sympathize with us, and due expression of their desires be forwarded to senators, representatives, and other public officials, advising them that the entire constituency of the Southern Convention, aided by sympathizing friends from every part of the country, are united in one sacred effort for the deliverance of a man of God who, by his unselfish devotion and his unflinching courage, has endeared himself to all who are familiar with his history; that for this purpose we ask that the Baptists throughout the South will, through their respective churches and other organizations, make contributions to a fund providing for the expense attending efforts for his relief, but more especially as a tangible expression of their sympathy for him and for his deliverance from the dangers environing him.

How speedily and graciously has God responded to the prayers of his people for their brother in affliction! While these lines are writing Dr. Diaz is on the sea, bound, as were the Pilgrim Fathers centuries ago, for our land of priceless personal liberty, universal political equality, absolute, joyous, unrestricted religious freedom.

But must the work, so nobly and gloriously begun in Cuba by Diaz, cease now and come to naught through the commotions and wars which at present agitate this promising island? Let us, in all earnestness and faith, pray the great God of the harvest that such may not be the calamity so widely feared. What has been thus far accomplished for Christ's cause in Cuba is, as one in

close touch with the work has said, "but the beginning
of this region's evangelization."

With all these triumphs, the great mass of spiritual destitution
has but been touched. Compared with the dense population,
numerically, the Christian Baptists are but a feeble folk. There
has been but a single sun ray piercing the rotten muck. All that
has passed has been but a work of preparation. But where in the
history of modern missions was there ever such a beginning as
this? Compare Judson's seven years of waiting with Diaz' first
service, memorable to him because his own fanatic mother was
the first trophy of the Spirit's power. . .

Only a beginning, yet a beginning like the dawn of its open
tropic land, without the long-extended twilight, with slow creep-
ing of ruddy hues upon the eastern horizon. As the sun seems to
leap with the ardor and vitality of youth from amidst the gloomy
curtains of the nights into the glory and splendor of a magnificent
day, the gospel has shone upon the gem of the Caribbean.

The future looks dark.   Clouds, heavy and ominous,
partly obscure the firmament of our hope.   As the
writer pens this page, there is handed him the following letter (with a few verbal changes) from one of
the "faithful" of Cuba :

HAVANA, April 24, 1896.

Very soon now we shall be entirely without ministers. Dr. Diaz
is the last one here, and he leaves to-morrow, ordered away by
the government. A week ago Sunday he baptized three girls from
the school, and there was an unusually good turnout; the following Thursday, at five A. M., he and his brother were arrested, his
house searched, but nothing found. Dr. Diaz offered the officials
coffee. After they partook they escorted both to the police station, where they were put into solitary confinement with a chair
to sit on. On Friday A. M. Mr. Porta found his way to them and
sent a message by the guard, and the reply through the guard was,

two cots and breakfast for two; until then they had had no food.
After the fou th day the family could see them at twelve P. M. and
yesterday. The following Thursday we had our last prayer meeting in the church. On Wednesday, five P. M., Dr. Diaz and his
brother were turned out of jail. The consul, of course, was em-
ployed and telegrams sent to the States. It is over now. I shall
be glad to see them outside the Morro Castle. Nothing has been
proved against them; no one thinks it is a political affair; but
rather the persecutions of the church in disguise.

Well, the meetings are closed and nothing has ever been sadder
here, except Dr. Diaz' father's funeral. It was a deluge of tears,
beginning with the pastor. He has sterling qualities and knows
no fear. I was surprised to hear him talk in such a fearless way.
He mentioned that the same police that had imprisoned him before were present. They were in disguise, and he recognized
them in passing up the aisle and took them to a better seat, just
behind us, and you may not believe it, they sang. Had I known
or suspected who they were, I would have given them my hymn
book, the words were all so appropriate; it was heartrending; we all
felt terribly. I will send you the hymns. The chapter was Acts
20. Every verse of each hymn seemed to have a sermon in it. All
was so kind, such persuasion, so much loving advice for his people
from our pastor during his absence, such entreaties not to aban-
don their faith or church associations. Poor Mr. Porta is devoted
to Dr. Diaz; all were very much affected; one handkerchief was
not sufficient to absorb the flood of tears.

April 25. Since I began this I hear that Dr. Diaz has ob-
tained permission to remain until Wednesday to finish all his busi-
ness. I don't feel safe until I see him on the boat. He was col-
lared again Thursday evening before service to sign some paper.
Two policemen took him as if he were some thief. I hope that
there is something better in store for him and that his work may
be doubly blessed in the future. All the time his wife and mother
and sisters were tearing about town in their anxiety about him,
never one word was uttered against the authorities. They are all
brave women. Asuncion lost her head, and walked from one end

of Havana to the other trying to catch sight of her brothers, thinking that she had only walked a short distance.   When Mr. Porta
told her how far it was, she said, "No wonder I felt exhausted."
Alfreda's wife and her five children will live in Rev. Mr. Cova's
house, and she and Mrs. Diaz, the widow, will take charge of the
school; but Miss Diaz and the girls live at Buenos Aires at the
hospital, and take their boarding scholars with them and have a
school there, and Miss Diaz' sisters live in Neptuno Street and
keep up that school, so three schools are all that will be left.   Mrs.
Diaz and Asuncion will make an attempt at mission work in some
of the neighboring families.   Mr. Cova is established in Tampa,
working among the Cubans and Spanish there.   The Rev. Mr.
O'Halloran in Key West; in the same way Mr. Klejo is also in
Key West.   Mr. Porta, Mr. Valdy, and Cruto remain here, and
we will follow Dr. Diaz' advice and meet as often as possible to
have service in different localities.   Singing is suppressed.   The
cemetery we shall keep open as long as possible.   I think I have
given you all the news of importance; in fact there is not much
left to talk about.   Carlos Diaz was sent with Mr. O'Halloran to
attend school at Key West.   Sincerely yours,

T.

Such words as these from a simple, trusting, timor-
ous heart move our hearts to renewed interest and sympathy, and call forth more earnest supplication that the
loving Father above will return to the poor, persecuted
Baptists their brother and leader from whom they have
been so cruelly separated, and thus impart to them joy
for mourning and the garment of praise for the spirit of
heaviness.

www.ingramcontent.com/pod-product-compliance
Lightning Source LLC
Chambersburg PA
CBHW021453090426
42739CB00009B/1742